T0077096

Displaying Information

Maps, Maps, Maps!

by Kelly Boswell

CAPSTONE PRESS
a capstone imprint

A+ Books are published by Capstone Press,
1710 Roe Crest Drive, North Mankato, Minnesota 56003
www.capstonepub.com

Copyright © 2014 by Capstone Press, a Capstone imprint. All rights reserved. No part of this publication may be reproduced in whole or in part, or stored in a retrieval system, or transmitted in any form or by any means, electronic, mechanical, photocopying, recording, or otherwise, without written permission of the publisher.

Library of Congress Cataloging-in-Publication Data
Boswell, Kelly.
 Maps, maps, maps! / by Kelly Boswell.
    pages cm. — (A+ books : Displaying information)
 Includes index.
 Summary: "Introduces types of maps and how they are used"—Provided by publisher.
 ISBN 978-1-4765-0262-5 (library binding)
 ISBN 978-1-4765-3339-1 (paperback)
 ISBN 978-1-4765-3343-8 (ebook PDF)
 1. Maps—Juvenile literature. I. Title.
 GA105.6.B66 2014
 912—dc23   2012050515

Editorial Credits
Kristen Mohn, editor; Juliette Peters, designer; Marcie Spence, media researcher; Charmaine Whitman, production specialist

Photo Credits
Capstone Studio: Karon Dubke, cover (middle), 1, 4 (left), 4–5, 6, 7, 8, 9, 15, 16, 21, 24–25, 32; iStockphoto: BirdsofPrey, 10, CEFutcher, 20, Rubberball, 14; Shutterstock: Alex and Anna, 18–19, bahri altay, cover (bottom), Debu55y, 12–13, Diana Rich, 4 (right), Haizul, 3, 5, 32, jorgen mcleman, 17, Pedro Nogueira, cover (bottom), Seamartini Graphics, cover (top), Stawek, 26–27, Teschanko Irina, cover (bottom), Tribalium, 29, wavebreakmedia, 22–23

Note to Parents, Teachers, and Librarians
This Displaying Information book uses full color photographs and a nonfiction format to introduce the concept of maps. This book is designed to be read aloud to a pre-reader or to be read independently by an early reader. Photographs help listeners and early readers understand the text and concepts discussed. The book encourages further learning by including the following sections: Table of Contents, Glossary, Read More, Internet Sites, and Index. Early readers may need assistance using these features.

Table of Contents

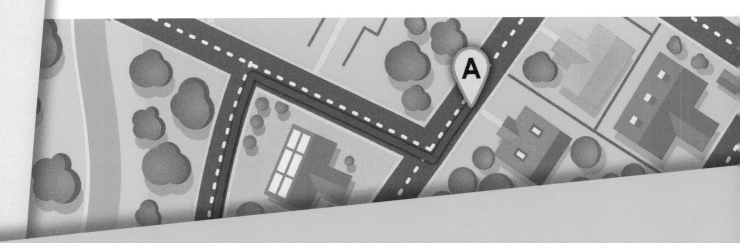

Maps All Around

Look around and you'll see maps. There are maps in parks, shopping malls, and museums. There are maps of your town or city, maps of your country, and maps of the world.

Keep Right at Main Street

1/2 mi

1:30
15.5 mi
ETA 1:45 pm

11:47

MENU

Maps can show you where things are and how to get where you want to go.

Brady is making a city. He has houses, buildings, roads, a river, and a train track in his city.

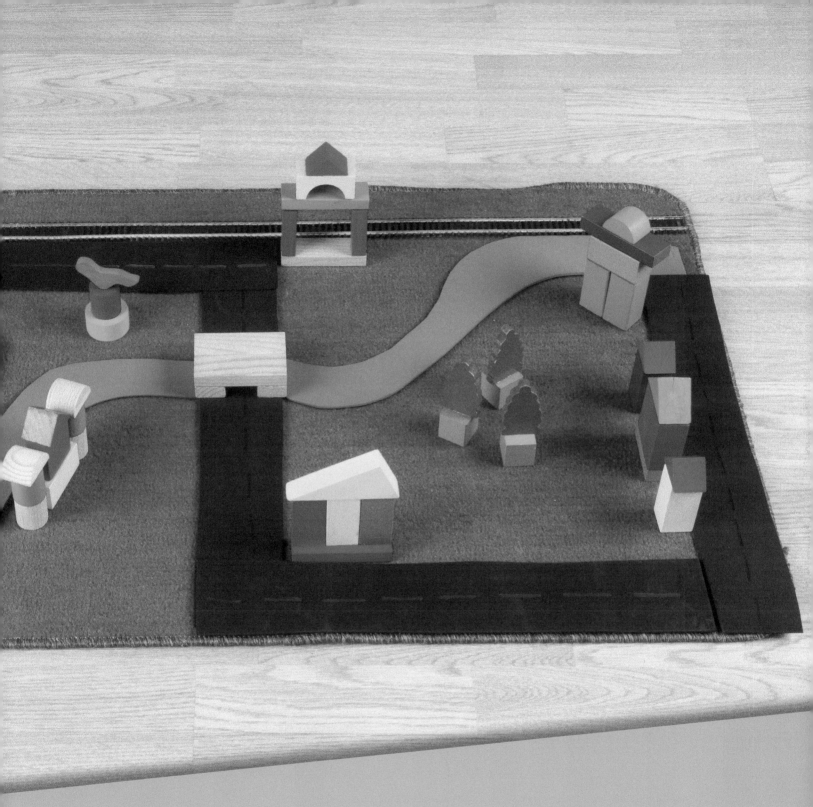

When he stands up, he can see the city from above.

Maps show things from above too.

Brady makes a map to show the parts of his city.

He labels each part.

Now he needs a title for the map. The title tells others what the map is showing.

Brady City

train tracks

road

river

pond

Map Symbols

Today Fran's family is at an amusement park. They want to take a balloon ride and go on the Ferris wheel. First they need lunch.

They use a map to find out which way to go.

There are symbols at the side
or bottom of most maps.

Each symbol stands for something on the map.
The box that shows these symbols is called a key
or a legend. It explains what the symbols mean.

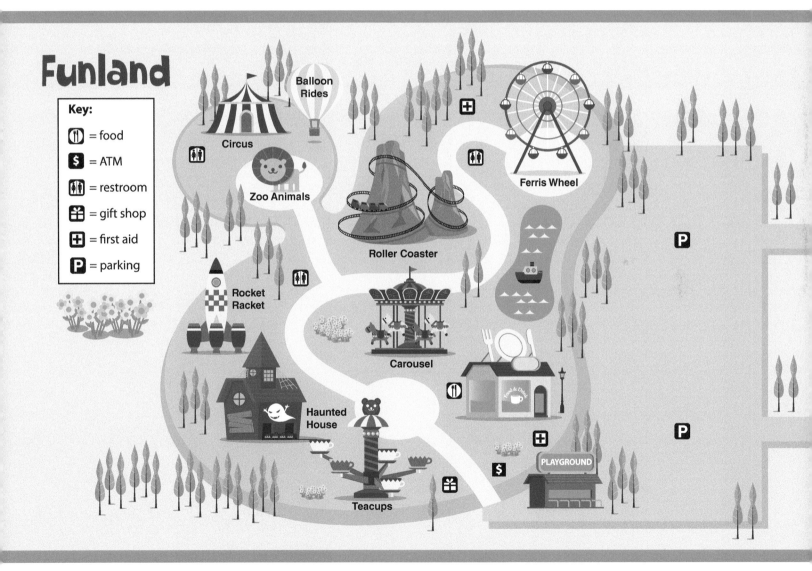

Where can they eat lunch?

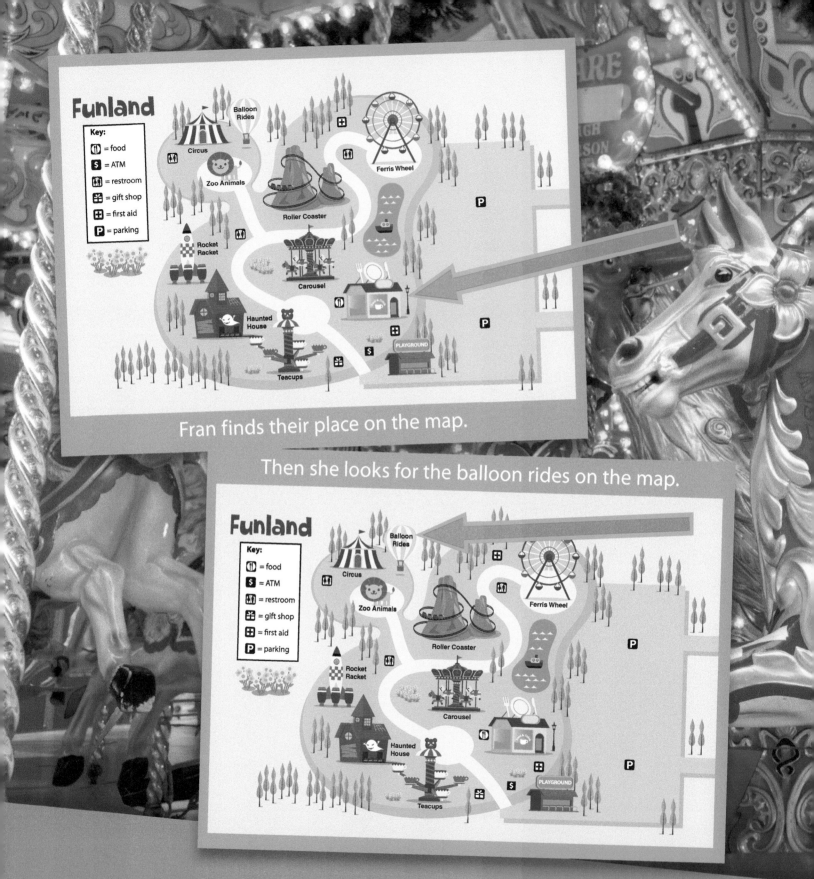

Fran finds their place on the map.

Then she looks for the balloon rides on the map.

They want to get from here to there.

Funland

Key:
- 🍴 = food
- 💲 = ATM
- 🚻 = restroom
- 🎁 = gift shop
- ➕ = first aid
- 🅿 = parking

Balloon Rides

Circus

Zoo Animals

Ferris Wheel

Roller Coaster

Rocket Racket

Carousel

Haunted House

Teacups

Food & Drink

PLAYGROUND

What will they pass on their way to the balloon ride?
How will they get to the Ferris wheel next?

Compass Rose

Jordan and her dad are planning a nature hike. They want to see the waterfall. A map can help. It shows a trail to the waterfall.

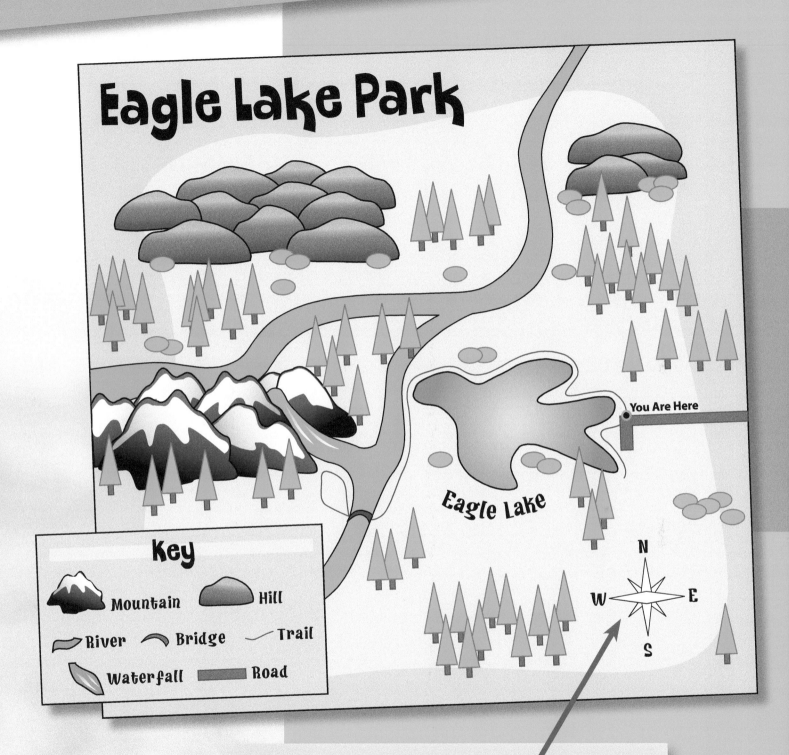

This symbol is called a compass rose. It shows north, south, east, and west on the map. The waterfall is to the west.

Let's go!

Jade has been invited to play at Kayla's house. A computer can help her find the way. Jade's mom types in their home address and Kayla's address.

The computer makes a map of Jade's town. The red line shows a route from their house to Kayla's house. It will take 10 minutes to drive there.

Political Maps

Some maps show a whole country.

A political map shows the boundaries between states or countries.

MINNESOTA

WISCONSIN
St. Paul

MICHIGAN
Lansing

IOWA
Des Moines

Lincoln

ILLINOIS
Springfield

INDIANA
Indianapolis

OHIO
Columbus

Madison

Topeka

Jefferson City

MISSOURI

OKLAHOMA

Oklahoma
City

ARKANSAS
Little Rock

LOUISIANA

Baton
Rouge

ustin

Jackson

MISSISSIPPI

ALABAMA
Montgomery

Atlanta

GEORGIA

Tallahassee

FLORIDA

TENNESSEE

Nashville

KENTUCKY

Frankfort

WEST
VIRGINIA
Charleston

VIRGINIA
Richmond

Raleigh

NORTH
CAROLINA

Columbia

SOUTH
CAROLINA

VERMONT
Montpelier

MAINE
Augusta

NEW HAMPSHIRE
Concord

MASSACHUSETTS
Boston

Albany

NEW YORK

PENNSYLVANIA
Harrisburg

RHODE ISLAND
Providence

CONNECTICUT
Hartford

NEW JERSEY
Trenton

DELAWARE
Dover

MARYLAND
Annapolis
Washington, D.C.

N

W   E

S

The capital cities are
marked with a star. Can
you find the capital of the
United States on this map?

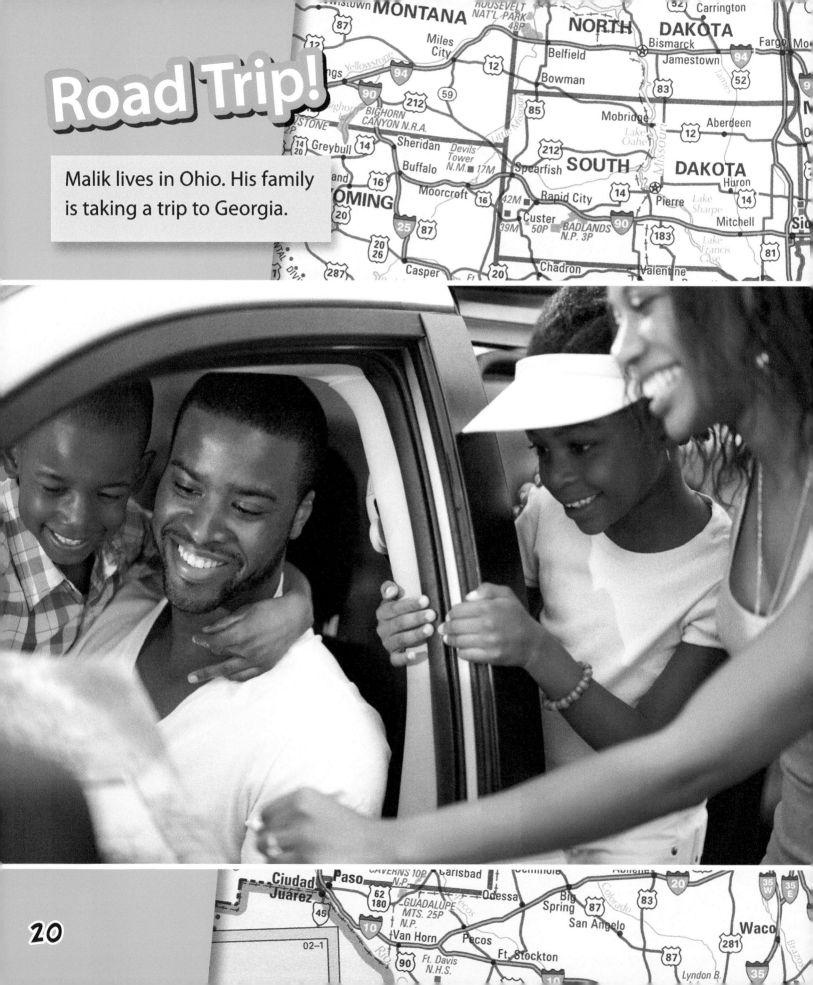

Road Trip!

Malik lives in Ohio. His family is taking a trip to Georgia.

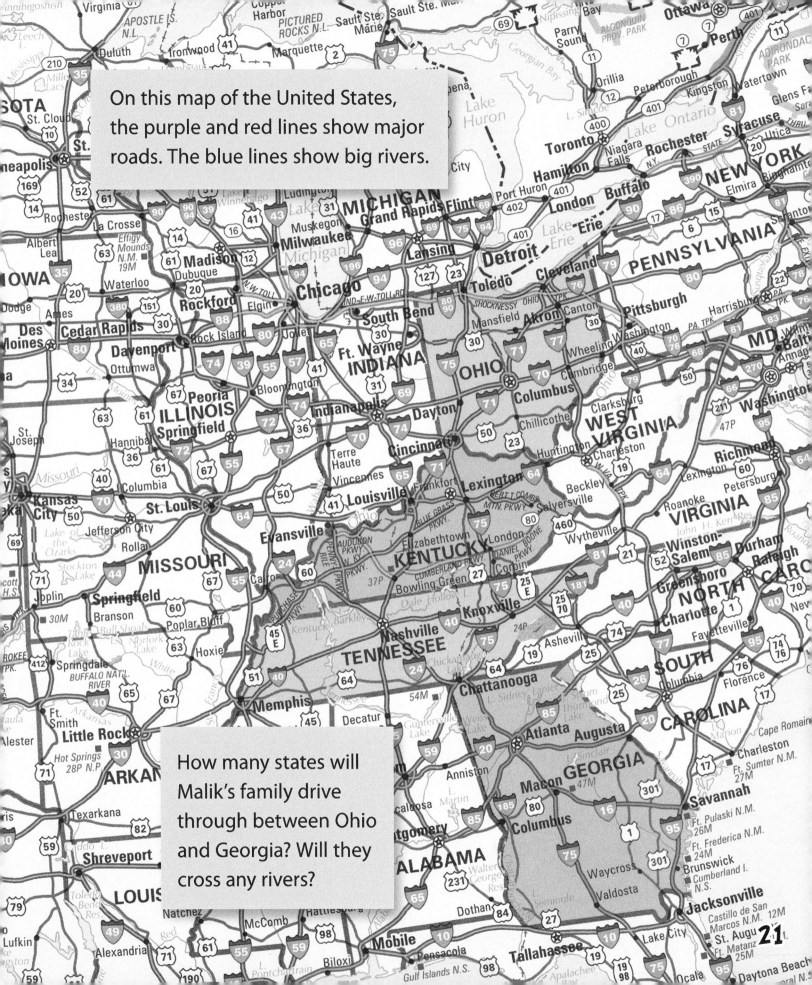

On this map of the United States, the purple and red lines show major roads. The blue lines show big rivers.

How many states will Malik's family drive through between Ohio and Georgia? Will they cross any rivers?

21

Globes

A globe is a special kind of map.

It is shaped like Earth. It shows the whole world.

Wow! Look at all of the blue on the globe. Blue shows the water that covers Earth. There is more water than land.

Carson lives in Canada. His pen pal, Bruno, lives in Brazil.

Here is Canada.

Here is Brazil.

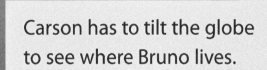

Carson has to tilt the globe
to see where Bruno lives.

World Map

North America

South America

A world map is another way to look at the whole world at once. When you look at this map, you can see the seven continents that make up our world.

Europe

Asia

Africa

Australia

Where is your continent?

Antarctica

Fun With Maps

Maps help us get around town and around the world. They tell us where to turn right or left, east or west.

What else can you use maps for? Finding treasure!

Where will a map take you?

Glossary

boundary—a border that separates one area from another

capital—a city that is an official center of government

compass rose—a label that shows direction on a map

continent—one of Earth's seven large masses of land

key—a list or chart that explains symbols on a map or graph; a key is sometimes called a legend

route—the road or course followed to get somewhere

symbol—a design or an object that stands for something else

Critical Thinking Using the Common Core

1. Study the map on pages 18 and 19. Use the compass rose to tell which states are to the north and to the south of Kansas. (Key Ideas and Details)

2. Look at the map on page 11. Locate the gift shop on the map. Explain how you found the gift shop. (Craft and Structure)

3. Draw a map of your neighborhood. What parts of a map will you include on your map? Use the map on page 8 as an example. (Integration of Knowledge and Ideas)

Read More

Greve, Meg. *Maps Are Flat, Globes Are Round*. Little World Geography. Vero Beach, Fla.: Rourke Pub., 2010.

Jackson, Kay. *Ways to Find Your Way: Types of Maps*. Map Mania. Mankato, Minn.: Capstone Press, 2008.

Olien, Rebecca. *Map Keys*. Rookie Read-About Geography. New York: Children's Press, 2012.

Internet Sites

FactHound offers a safe, fun way to find Internet sites related to this book. All of the sites on FactHound have been researched by our staff.

Here's all you do:

Visit *www.facthound.com*

Type in this code: 9781476502625

Check out projects, games and lots more at
www.capstonekids.com

Index

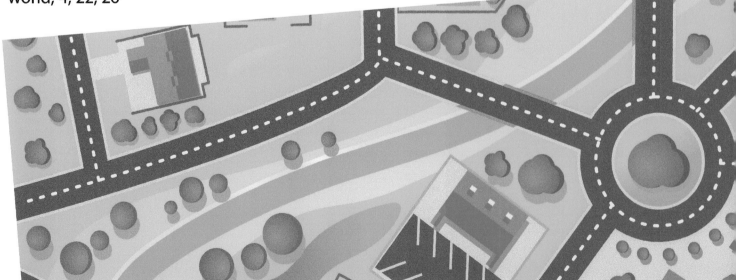